T0064077

9 The to 5
Property
Millionaire

How you can be a millionaire property
investor while working 9 to 5

BK Khoo

PARTRIDGE
A Penguin Random House Company

To order additional copies of this book, contact
Toll Free 800 101 2657 (Singapore)
Toll Free 1 800 81 7340 (Malaysia)
orders.singapore@partridgepublishing.com

www.partridgepublishing.com/singapore

For Jayden

Contents

Foreword

W e all have a "love affair" with property. For a start, we all live in one, whether we actually own it or not. It's a topic of constant fascination with the media with property prices frequently making headline news. It is closely related to each and every one of us.

What about property as an investment? We've all heard that holding property is a good thing because it is "bricks and mortar". It goes up in value and creates cash flow income. It provides housing solutions to tenants and a legacy to our children. For a lot of people, owning a property is the first step in creating wealth as we were often told since we were kids that we should finish our education, get a job so we could get on the property ladder. When my grandmother passed away while I was a teenager, I became the sole heir, amongst all her grandchildren, to her property as her eldest grandson. Although this injustice would be difficult to fathom by today's standard, my grandmother's wish was for me to be the first male in the family to finish college and go to university. Needless to say it did result in a rather hostile feud not dissimilar to that in the 80s TV drama *Dynasty*! Eventually when I bought my own property in London in 1997, it made me £38,000 in less than two years on the back of a property boom, which began my own property journey. If I hadn't sold it then, my profit would stand at more than half a million pounds today!

Having invested in property and mentored thousands of people around the world in the past decade, one thing I've discovered is that people are often confused about the subject. Is it a good time to get into property? Is it risky? Where do I start looking? For beginners, it's always a question of how it would be possible for anyone to be in a 9 to 5 job to get started in property. While there are countless number of books on the subject of property investment, none has particularly stood out that provides a practical guide showing people how to get out of the "rat race" from the personal experience and perspective of someone who has "walked the talk". Back in 2012 during one of my seminars in Kuala Lumpur, I met a dynamic and determined young investor called BK Khoo who had already achieved some success in investing in property part time. From our conversation, I learned that he was working for a tobacco factory as a manager facing the imminent prospect of being made redundant. Eventually when it did happen, rather than being fazed by the lack of employment, BK stepped up his game and turned full time in property. On my last visit in Malaysia in late 2013, I was delighted to hear that he was telling his story through his first book "*The 9 to 5 Property Millionaire*" and was surprised and flattered to be asked to write a foreword for it. For me, a book that teaches the knowledge of how to invest in property whilst in a job is well overdue, as it shares my unshakable belief that ordinary people need to know that there is a *choice* besides working 9 to 5 trading time for money; putting money aside in their savings only to be eroded by inflation; contributing towards their pension only to find that they are unable to retire at retirement age and accepting what the Asian cultural belief that one's life and wealth are down to fate and cannot be altered.

The *9 to 5 Property Millionaire* is a must-have guide for anyone wishing to build a profitable property portfolio alongside their 9 to 5 jobs or give up their jobs to become a full-time investor. The wealth of information is invaluable to new and experienced alike. There are chapters on property millionaire mindset, strategic planning and step-by-step practical implementations. It discusses the fundamentals of asset building using "good debts" and how one could leverage on other people's time and resources by building a winning property team. In my opinion, the knowledge in this book is an absolute gem! Read it, digest it and take massive action on it and it would pave the way for anyone wishing to build a successful career in property with confidence and competence.

Vincent Wong, MBA

Co-founder of Wealth Dragons
International speaker and co-author of
"*Step by Step Guides to Lease Options*"
"*Property Millionaire Secrets*" and
"*Your Wealth Dragon Unleashed*".

Testimonials

"*T*he book has an "*intimate*" quality to it—*the contents flow like a conversation with a friend written in an easy to follow and very personalized manner, devoid of jargons and technical terms. It is akin to having completed Property 101 minus the heavy reading—perfect for beginners like me. Highly recommended.*"—Lim Toh Seng, Manager Compliance

"*It's a really great book for a new property investor, explaining A-Z of all you need to know before you start the cycle. I found it simple, not many jargons that sometimes confuse you, and a book that anyone and everyone can understand. Great initiative! Well done!*"—Subashni, Freelance Trainer

"*You'll discover a whole new world of opportunities and possibilities in just 15 mins. Excellent easy read for the aspiring millionaires!*"—Angie Lim, Marketing Manager

I must say BK has made property investments sound simple & straightforward. To me, this book is suitable for new kids on the block who do not have idea on property investments or like people like me who want to invest but have not taken any action. Truly inspiring!—Tan Seow Eng, Manager Finance.

"*The Author was a colleague of mine. When he said to me that he would write about his true passion, it was very clear from the outset that his thought processes and rationale would easily make for compelling reading.*

I've watched with fascination and admiration through the years on how the author has time and time again out-thought problems and situations, most importantly, presented it in a simple and easy to understand way. This ability, in my mind, is amply demonstrated in the book you read now.

The 9 to 5 millionaire has helped me simplify what is a terribly confusing and at best, frustrating endeavor. It's a reflection of the intellect that made our lives a lot easier at work, and, now, will make yours easier when you look to invest."—Nick Goh, QA Manager

Acknowledgement

First and foremost, if you are reading this, then I would like to thank you for picking up this book. If you are looking to achieve more financial success in your life, then please continue reading as I am sharing what I have learnt as I went through out looking for financial success in my life through property investment. I wish you the very best in your financial future.

I also would like to thank my wife, Li Lian, for being my partner and best friend in life. To my family, especially my parents, parents-in-law and brother, for their support and advice in my endeavors. To the Wealth Dragons, John Lee and Vincent Wong, thank you for mentoring me along my journey to financial success. To Nick, for being the sounding board and source of many ideas. And to everyone else, who have contributed to my success, I thank you all too.

Why I wrote this book . . .

I wrote this book because I think it is important for everyone out there, especially employees, to invest. I hope to inspire employees to start investing for a brighter future for themselves and their loved ones. I would also love to inspire business owners and entrepreneurs who are looking to start in property investments. I am sure that most of the topics I cover would reach out to non-employees too.

When I first lost my job on my wedding day in 2009, I was not investing and the only safety net I had was the savings that I had in my bank account, which was not much at the time. However, I knew I had to make a change and took it one step at a time. I must admit, it was not necessarily easy as sacrifices needed to be made along the way, but after achieving some success, the sacrifices were definitely worth it.

Over time, I realized that many employees were like me when I first started working, very much focused on climbing the corporate ladder and were not investing. Everyone had their own reason. Some told me they did not have the time, others said they did not know enough or did not dare to take risks. Whatever your reason may be, I sincerely hope you can take the first step, which is to learn. Taking the first step is always the hardest. Similar to a rocket trying to leave earth to outer space, you need a lot of energy to break away from earth's gravity field.

Interestingly enough, I noticed that the concepts and process used in a multi-national company are very valid when investing, especially in property. Also, soft-skills that I learnt through my job became useful to me in my property investments too. For example, I had the honor of managing a team later on in my career and the things I learnt from managing my team at work also could be applied to managing my tenants.

In all honesty, if I was not told by my company that I had to leave them in 2013, I would have stayed with my company as I truly enjoyed what I did for a living. However, since the decision was already made for me by the company, I have now decided that I will now set off on my own and leave the world of employment. I hope that by sharing my story, I can inspire others to take their first steps into investments.

1) The Shocking Truth about having a job!

Why you must invest in property while having a job

When I was growing up, I was told that it was important for me to go to school, study hard, get a degree or diploma and get a job. Getting a job was the ultimate goal, so that you could have a steady income until the time of your retirement. This would then allow you to start a family and have kids, who then would ultimately get a job and take care of you when you retire. It was the basics of life and for many years, I accepted it without question.

I was pretty well set. I went to school and did reasonably well in the major exams. I graduated with honors from a local university. And most importantly, I got a job at a multi-national company. So far, so good. Everything was going as planned. Until one day, I lost my job.

I remember that day well. It was a Friday and my wife and I were actually on leave getting ready for one of the biggest moments of our lives—our wedding reception in my home town. Sometime that evening, I got a call from my boss informing me that that day would be my last day of service with the company and as I was on leave I could come in next Monday and collect my belongings. There goes my honeymoon . . .

How could this be? I was doing everything an employee was supposed to be doing. I was achieving results, making improvements and

I even got promoted as recognition for my achievements. Yet, the reality was, the company was not doing well and was becoming bankrupt. And as a result, had to close the factory I was working in and retrench all employees.

I was disappointed. The job did not bring me any security. If anything at all, I was even more insecure after being retrenched as I needed to get a job fast. I had some savings, enough for a few months but I did not know how long it would take for me to get a new job. Other companies were also retrenching employees at the time. Fortunately for me, I managed to get a job within 3 months.

The most important thing I learnt out of this whole experience is that having a job is not a secure as it seems! The truth is you are employed as long as the company needs you. When a company ceases to need you, it would not care too much if you are financially stable or if you are able to survive without a job. I know of many people who run into financial difficulties the moment they lose their jobs. So, rather than complain about it or worry about if it happens, we need to take responsibility and be proactive to prepare ourselves.

So what should you do?

Very often, most of us have many contingency plans mapped out in life and whilst on our jobs. We keep umbrellas at home, in the car and in the office, just in case it rains. It's what we are taught to do when planning activities. And yet, most of us, especially employees, only have a single source of income. Isn't it interesting that for one of the most important aspects of our life, we do not have a contingency plan?

I have worked for two companies in my working career and I have never resigned. The first company I worked for went bankrupt and the second re-structured its operations and as a result I (among others) were retrenched. The first time I lost my job, I had no choice but to immediately go out searching for a job. The second time it happened, I was ready for it and now am free to do pretty much whatever I want.

After losing my job the first time, I decided that I had to look for another source of income. A financial contingency plan. As I was still an employee at the time, and did not have the time for 2 jobs at a time, I started looking at investments. After much research on the various investment vehicles, I settled on properties.

Interestingly enough, I did not set out to become a millionaire through properties. All I wanted was to have some properties for investment as a secondary source of income. Now enough about me, what about you? Do you have your contingency plan in place? What are you going to do about it? I hope that by sharing my story and knowledge you can set up your own contingency plan and become a property millionaire along the way.

Why Property Investments?

Out of the many property investment vehicles in the world, why property? There are a number of criteria that I looked at when deciding on property over the other investment vehicles. I personally chose property investments based on the following criteria. These criteria needed to complement the fact that I was an employee with fixed working hours. I am sure it would also suit you and any other employee out there as our circumstances would be similar.

Effort Required

Each investment type requires different amount of effort required during both start-up and during managing the investment. Properties are a type of investment that suits employees as it involves more effort during the start-up, which is a one-off effort when you are purchasing a property and significantly less effort when managing the property. This one-off effort can be done on weekends or after working hours, so an employee does not need to take leave to get it done.

Potential Returns

Property investments are physical assets with value that increases over time and are also able to generate cash flow by collecting rental from tenants. In other words, there are two ways of generating returns from properties—capital gains and rental returns. This then basically creates additional income streams for you.

Capital Gains

Properties are very much certain of having capital appreciation over time as they are a physical and tangible asset. There are 3 main reasons why property prices will always appreciate over time.

(i) **Scarcity of land + Increase in population**—The biggest driver for the constant increase in property prices is the fact that raw land is becoming scarce. At the same time, the population is growing every year. As more and more land is developed over time to meet the demand created by the increasing population, whatever land that remains undeveloped will become more expensive.

(ii) **Inflation of Material Prices**—Property prices will also go up as long as there is inflation. With inflation, prices of raw material required for development of property will go up. And as the price of raw materials go up, so must the price of properties.

(iii) **Increase in Cost of Labor**—Another reason is the cost of labor that constantly will increase. Quite simply, everyone is looking for a raise every year. And for property developers to give their employees and business partners a raise, they would have to also increase property prices from time to time.

Rental Returns

Properties are also able to generate rental returns as there are many people that prefer to rent instead of buy properties. Some examples of such people are expatriates who are on short term assignments, students who need to stay near their place of education, fresh graduates who are just starting work, and employees who have just relocated due to job requirements.

Leverage

Financial institutions, including banks, are quite willing to lend money for property loans at low interest rates as properties are tangible assets that cannot simply disappear. They do not lend for other common investments such as stocks or mutual funds. On top of that, you also have the flexibility of deciding how much you would like to borrow for the investment. By leveraging on other people's money, you are able to generate more return on investment than if you were to only use your own money. And it allows you to spread your risk across different properties, that you do not carry all your eggs (your cash) in one basket (property). It is always better to have your eggs in different baskets.

A simple example to illustrate the advantages of leveraging on bank loans to invest in property is as follows . . .

	Cash Purchase	Purchase with 90% loan
Purchase Price (RM)	200,000	200,000
Cash Payment (RM)	200,000	20,000
Loan from Bank (RM)	0	180,000
After 5 years, the value of the property appreciates to RM 300,000 and you decide to sell . . .		
Selling Price (RM)	300,000	300,000
Capital Gain (RM)	100,000	100,000
Return on Investment	50%	500%

For scenario A, the return on investment is 50%—not bad . . . but you would have to commit RM200,000 cash, which is not likely for an average employee.

For Scenario B, the return of investment is 500%! 5 times the cash that was put down up front. And it is definitely realistic to be able to save up RM20,000 than RM 200,000.

Stability

Properties are very stable investments and are also very predictable when compared to investments such as stocks or foreign exchange. The prices of property do not fluctuate very much and it can also be a forgiving investment if you "over-paid" as long as you hold it until the price appreciates sufficiently. Having a steady job complements this very well as a steady paycheck supports any need to hold on to properties.

2) Think you are ready? You sure?

Know the basics for you to be the next 9-5 property millionaire

If you want to be successful, you need to prepare yourself that you are ready to take the opportunity when it appears. In property investment there are three main foundations that you need to have before you start investing. Without having these foundations you could end up making costly mistakes.

The example that is quite commonly used when talking about foundations is the example of building a house. In the case of property investments, the house would look like this . . .

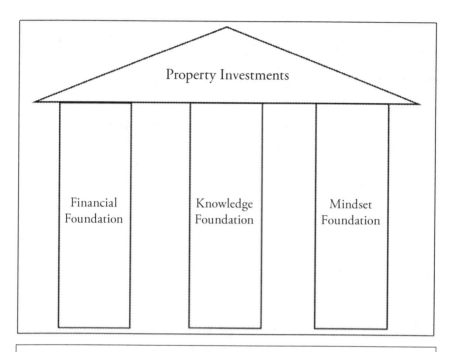

The Standard Operating Procedure (SOP) to success is really just it . . . S.O.P.

Success = Opportunity + Preparation

To be successful in anything that you do, you need to be prepared. There is a saying that goes "you make your own luck", which is not very far from the truth. For example, if you think a lottery winner is lucky, have you considered that he or she was prepared to take the opportunity by buying that lottery ticket in the first place?

Financial Foundations

Properties are high cost investments. They require a lot of capital and also in cases where you have a loan, require cash flow for repayments. As such, it is very important to be financially ready before investing. To be financially ready, you would need to know your current financial status, which comprises of two main indicators. These two main indicators are your net worth and your monthly cash flow.

Net Worth

Your net worth is basically the difference between the assets that you own and the liabilities that you have.

$$\text{Net Worth = Assets - Liabilities}$$

One simple way is to set up a spreadsheet, such as MS Excel, to record all your assets and liabilities. Your assets should include your properties, vehicles, retirement funds (i.e. EPF), mutual funds, stocks, fixed deposits, and cash in hand. Liabilities should include any loans (whether from banks or other financial institutions), and credit card debts.

If you are currently having a negative net worth, you should first work on getting it to a positive net worth before investing. Having a negative net worth basically means you owe others more than what you own. In which case, should you have no job, you would be very close to bankruptcy as you would be unable to repay all your debts even if you sold off all your assets.

If you are currently having a positive net worth, you are in good shape—but you still need to assess your cash flow before you start investing.

The 2 types of Assets

There are 2 basic types of assets, which are appreciating assets and depreciating assets. An appreciating asset is an asset that goes up in value over time, whereas a depreciating asset is an asset that loses value over time.

Property is a good example of an appreciating asset as the value of a property goes up over time.

A car is an example of a depreciating asset as the value of the car decreases over time.

So when analyzing your net worth, you should also take note of how many of your assets are appreciating and depreciating. Ideally, you should have more appreciating assets than depreciating assets.

The 2 types of Debts

There are 2 basic types of debts, which are good debt and bad debt. A good debt is one a debt where you are able to generate profit, whereas a bad debt is one where you end up losing money.

An example of a good debt is a loan on a property where you are receiving rental that is more than the monthly loan installment, which generates profit for you.

An example of a bad debt is a car loan as you end up paying interest on an asset that is losing value every day.

So when analyzing your net worth, you should also take note of how much of your debt is good debt and how much is bad debt. You need to work on increasing your good debt and eliminating your bad debt.

Example:
Below are a list of assets and liabilities for Mr. X

Assets	Value	Liabilities	Value
Property #1	100,000	Home Loan #1	70,000
Property #2	150,000	Home Loan #2	100,000
Car	50,000	Car Loan	30,000
Shares	50,000		
Cash in Hand	50,000		
Total	400,000	Total	200,000

Therefore, the Net Worth of Mr. X = Assets - Liabilities
= 400,000 - 200,000
= 200,000

Monthly Cash Flow

Your monthly cash flow is the difference between your income and expenses within one month.

Cash Flow = Income - Expenses

Similar to Net Worth, a simple way to track your monthly cash flow is to record it in a spreadsheet. Your income should include all income that you receive in a month, including your basic salary, overtime pay, allowances, rental from properties. Any annual income such as bonuses can be averaged out and included. Your expenses should include all your monthly spending such as grocery shopping, rental, loan repayments, maintenance fees, taxes, insurance premiums.

If you are currently having a negative cash flow, you should first work on getting it to a positive cash flow before investing. Having a negative cash flow means you are spending more than what you are earning. This is not good even if you have positive net worth, because it sooner or later, your net worth will become negative.

If you are currently having a positive cash flow, you are in good shape—but do you have positive net worth? If you have negative net worth, don't worry, you are on the right track to go to a positive net worth.

If you have positive net worth and positive cash flow, congratulations! You can now start planning your budget for property investments!

Example:
Below are details of the monthly income and expense of Ms. Y

Income	Value	Expense	Value
Net Salary (less EPF & Tax)	4,000	Home Loan #1 Installment	800
Rental from Property	1,000	Home Loan #2 Installment	1,000
		Car Loan Installment	500
		Personal Insurance Premium	500
		Groceries & Food	1,000
		Utilities	200
		Daily Travel (Fuel, Toll, etc.)	500
Total	5,000	Total	4,500

Therefore, the Monthly Cash Flow of Ms. Y   = Income - Expense

$$= 5,000 - 4,500$$
$$= 500$$

Setting your budget

You must set your budget before your start any investments. This is to ensure that you are able to sustain your investment and make it successful.

The two key guidelines are

- The monthly installment of any loan you take must not cause your cash flow to change from positive to negative. For example, if you have a cash flow of RM 1,000 per month, and you take a loan with installment of RM 1,500, your cash flow would then become negative RM 500.
- You should not take on unnecessary liabilities to fund your investments. For example, if you don't have enough cash for the down payment, you should not take a personal loan to fund the down payment of a property. Doing this will most likely cause you to fall into negative net worth or put you into negative cash flow situation as well.

Knowledge Foundations

Knowledge is what you know and what you've learnt either through experience or education. So, it is very important to develop your knowledge so that you are able to come up with strategies that will make you successful in properties. This quote from Peter Drucker is very powerful and sums up what your Knowledge foundation can do for you.

Today knowledge has power. It controls access to opportunity and advancement.—Peter Drucker

Investing versus Speculating

It is very important that everyone understands the difference between investing and speculating as there is a rather blur line between the two. The real difference between investing and speculating is that one is done after proper assessment and the other is done without.

It is very easy to be a speculator as all you need is to listen for the latest rumors on what is a good buy, pay the money and hope for the best. Sometimes you do get lucky and profit, but when things go wrong, you may end up very much broke.

On the other hand, investing is about making informed decisions and taking calculated risks to achieve a profit. No matter what the latest rumor is, you can and will assess it to understand its risks and whether you are personally ready for it before investing. You can only do so if you know enough about the investment that you want to make.

The Number 1 Investment

The most important investment that anyone can make is actually the investment in oneself. Nobody is perfect and nobody knows everything. As such, it is important that we continuously invest in ourselves to keep on growing and creating opportunities.

It doesn't matter if you have no experience in properties or already have some experience in properties, you still need to continue learning. There are different ways of investing in yourself to build the knowledge such as through reading books, attending seminars and through action itself.

When you are starting out, you may want to read first, then attend seminars before actually taking action. Reading and attending seminars allow you to learn fast and leverage on the experiences of other successful investors to avoid making costly mistakes.

Taking action without sufficient preparation would be a very good lesson but also could be a very costly and painful lesson. If you already have some successful experience investing, great! Keep the momentum up and keep on learning, whether through your own experience or by leveraging on the experience of others.

Understanding Risk

Risk is something we face every day. Quite often we take risks without actually thinking about it. For example, did you consider the risk you are taking when you drive to work? Or how about when you last cut some fruits with a knife?

Taking the driving example, the government has put in place controls to ensure that all drivers are properly educated and given sufficient practice prior to being given a license to drive in public. Unfortunately, there is no such government control for property investments, which means we need to be proactive to educate ourselves and practice to make ourselves proficient at it.

Understanding the risk involved in each and every transaction is what will make you a successful investor. Once you are able to identify a property that is of low risk to you, then you are ready to invest.

Here are some examples of how to compare risk of different properties

Residential vs Commercial—Residential properties have a significantly larger market than Commercial properties. This is as everybody needs a place to stay (residential properties) but only businesses would have a use for commercial properties

Low-density vs High-density—Low-density developments are usually lower risk than high-density developments. This is because it is very likely that supply will be less than demand as there will be less units available for sale.

Urban vs Sub-urban—Properties in Urban areas are lower risk than properties in sub-urban areas. This usually is because demand is significantly greater in an urban area where people gravitate to for employment and business amongst other things.

Before Construction vs Completed—Buying completed properties are actually very low risk as you are able to judge with certainty then quality of the product and also the environment around the property. Buying before construction has the greatest risk of all, which is the developer going bankrupt and not being able to complete the construction! This doesn't happen very much now but it is still a risk.

Mindset Foundations

Last but not least of the foundations is the mindset foundation. This is as important if not more important than the other two foundations. I truly believe that if you have the right mindset, things will happen for you.

Know your reason

When you set out to invest, you need to know your reason for doing it. Having a purpose and a reason is what will drive you to success. It should not just be about making more money. Money is just a tool that should get you what you really want.

For example, do you want to be able to spend more time with your family? Or would you want to be able to travel the world? In both cases, money can help you achieve your goals. And in both cases, making money through property investments can help you achieve your goals.

Play to Win

Investing in properties is a game. And though this can be quite cliché, to be successful in any game, you need to play to win. If you want to be successful in life, you need to play to win. It is quite clear that anyone or any team that just plays defense will not win.

Spend some time and assess your own thoughts and actions and determine if you are someone who is playing to win or someone who is trying not to lose. If you are playing to win, you are always looking for the next opportunity to make something happen. And over time, people who play to win will win.

If you have not been playing to win all this while, do not worry. You can start now. Similar as to how you can develop your knowledge to be successful in property investments, you can also develop your mindset to be successful in property investments. There are many authors and experts out there who can help you develop the right mindset for success.

Emotions and Investments could explode if mixed

Another thing that is very important to note is that emotions and investments do not mix. Once you get emotional about an investment, you will make bad decisions. You need to be able to assess investments on their own merits without having any sentiment swaying your opinion.

For example, if you are looking a condominium to buy as an investment, and upon viewing it you suddenly fall in love with the place. Should you still buy it even though it makes no financial sense (have negative cash flow)? The answer is quite straight-forward, yet is it easy to walk away when faced with the decision?

Another example is when deciding to sell a property. Once you have decided to sell the property and have fixed an asking price, just go ahead and sell it. You should not be tempted by greed and keep asking for more. If you do, you could end up without a sale at all, which could then limit future opportunities that could come up in the future.

In both examples above, would you kick yourself if a great opportunity came up in the future but you were not financially ready as you either had spent the money on something that did not make financial sense or you had kept holding out for a better price on a property you should have sold?

It's Simple, but Never Easy

The last and yet most important part of your mindset should be the part where your mind is conditioned to take action. Taking action is always simple, but never easy. Sound confusing? Imagine you are trying to lose weight. What do you need to do? Eat healthy and exercise, right? That is simple isn't it? But is it so easy that everyone does it? Probably not.

So, to have any chance of success, you must take action. I stress again, you must take action! Sometimes, we strive too much for perfection that we end up not taking action. You need to balance having enough preparation with actually taking action. It is quite often that people get affected by "paralysis by analysis", which basically means one gets stuck analyzing something and ends being paralyzed and hence does not take action.

What you also need to realize is that in life, nothing comes for free and if something is too good to be true, it probably is. This is no get rich quick scheme. You will be facing challenges along the way, and you must face these challenges and overcome them if you are to be successful.

Most of the time, we need to start taking action and then figure things out as we go, making the necessary adjustments along the way. In the words of one of the most successful people around today.

Screw It, Let's Do It.—Sir Richard Branson

3) The Property Millionaire Game Plan

Strategies to building your million dollar property portfolio

To be successful in anything we do, we need to have a proper game plan. And this game plan consists of strategies that we use to bring us success. And to be successful, the game plan that we use needs to be specific to our current situation to bring the best results. We need to be flexible enough to change our strategies from time to time to ensure we keep winning!

Each strategy has its own advantages and disadvantages, which you need to learn and understand to be able to use them to your advantage. You will need to decide which strategy suits you best at any given point of time considering your financial, knowledge and mindset readiness. This chapter covers 5 basic strategies that you can consider using at the start of your investment journey.

Buy before construction and sell upon completion

Buying before completion has its risks, as was covered in a previous chapter, but if done correctly can also generate a lot of profit. The biggest advantage of buying before completion is that you are able to lock in the price today and sell at tomorrow's price.

It is also an easier entry investment as in Malaysia for those who cannot qualify for 90% loans, as the payments are done progressively. There is a fixed schedule of when developers can charge purchases based on the progress of the construction.

So if you select a new development in a mature location, you would be quite certain of making profit once the construction is completed. It is also better to buy developments that are of low density as then your competition to sell the property when it is completed is also slightly lower.

One of the risks of this strategy is the fact that you would not know how the end product looks like and if the quality is good. It must be noted though that most developers ensure they deliver good quality as they have reputations to keep.

Buy for Capital Appreciation

You could also invest in properties solely for capital appreciation. Though this may need a significant amount of cash flow, if you decide to buy with a loan, this strategy would be good if you prefer not to manage tenants.

For this strategy, the best type of property so far is either landed property, such as houses, irrespective if they are terrace, link, semi-detached or bungalows. Traditionally landed properties have always appreciated faster than high-rise properties. This is related to the fact that landed properties are actually built on land and not "up in the air".

You would also most likely want to keep the property for at least five years. This is because the Real Property Gains Tax (RPGT) in Malaysia is applicable up to five years. Which means if you decide to sell within 5 years, any profit you earn from the sale would be taxable. For now, this tax does not apply after five years, but do keep up to date for any changes as it would affect this strategy.

"Flipping"

Flipping is the strategy to generate capital gains in a short period of time. The two key parts of this strategy is first buying significantly below market value and second selling it for at least market value.

When done correctly one can generate large amounts of profit in a short time. Of course, you should only use this strategy when you have found a property that is significantly below market value and you are absolutely sure that you can sell it immediately after that for at least the market value.

Thing to note for this strategy is that properties are not usually sold below market value unless there is a specific reason. For example, the property may be in poor condition after not being occupied for many years. So, if you are able to fix up the property for less the difference of the market value and the price you are offered, you have a very good chance of using this strategy.

Buying to Rent

This strategy is a strategy that focuses on generating cash flow. You would identify a property with good rental yields to purchase and once you purchase it, you keep it forever. Residential properties sometime do offer good rental yields, but the best rental yields are in commercial properties.

You could decide to buy either before construction or completed properties for this strategy. However, should you buy before construction, you will be taking some amount of risk, unless you are very sure that the location has or will have high demand.

Buying completed properties, from the secondary market would be very low risk, especially if you are able to purchase it with a tenant already in place. However, on the flip side, not many owners would want to sell a property that is generating cash flow for them. If they did, they most likely would want a good price for it, which would mean you may not get good rental yield for a start until rental prices increase in the future.

This a good strategy for beginners as the risk is quite low, especially if you buy to rent properties that are completed in mature locations. If you can identify a property that fits this investment strategy, jump to get it.

Renting to Multiple Occupants

This strategy is really an extension of the Buy to Rent strategy. The key difference is instead of renting out the property as a whole to one tenant, you would rent all available rooms to a tenant each. What this usually does is generate more rental than renting all rooms out to a single tenant.

This strategy is good to implement on properties that are near schools, colleges or universities. Students prefer to rent rooms individually. Firstly they have their own privacy and secondly they are usually not interested in managing rooms they do not use. For example, a student would more likely want to rent a room for RM 400 than rent a three room apartment for RM 900 where they have to then look for and manage other tenants. So, should you rent out three rooms individually, you could earn RM 1,200 per month as compared to RM 900 per month, which is 33% more rent.

Of course, if you do use this strategy, then you would probably need to spend more time managing the property. But if you can generate that much more cash flow, would you not want to do it?

4) Mother said don't use other people's money . . . she's wrong!

How leveraging is key to your success

Actually, mother is correct when it comes to property that are meant for your own use. On the other hand, for investment properties, learning to invest with other people's money is the right thing to do.

As most of us do not have enough resources to buy property with cash, we would need to come up with financing strategies or leveraging. The most common way of financing is by borrowing from a financial institution, which is also known as a mortgage. However, there are also other ways to raise financing for property investments. This chapter covers 3 different ways to raise financing for your property investments.

Borrowing from a Financial Institution

Borrowing from a financial institution is the most common way of financing property investments. Most if not all of the financial institutions in Malaysia offer loan products for customers to buy property. Banks make up the majority of the financial institutions but in Malaysia there are financial institutions that are not banks, such as MBSB and AIA, which offer loans for property purchases.

Things to know when looking for a loan

Here are the key points that you need to understand and check when borrowing from a financial institution. You must understand these points to fully understand what you are signing up for before you actually sign the loan agreement. You must ensure the loan you are signing up for complements the strategy you are implementing. If you take the wrong loan for your strategy, you may end up losing money rather than making money.

- Type of Loan
- Base Lending Rate
- Interest Rates
- Tenure
- Lock-in Period

Type of loan

There are many different products being offered by the various financial institutions, but here is some information on the two most commons products being offered at the moment, the conventional loan and the flexi-loan.

Term Loan—The term loan is a straightforward loan product where the borrower has a fixed repayment amount and schedule. There is very limited flexibility offered with this product, which makes it very good for you if you are the type of person who needs some kind of rigidity to help you stay disciplined. In most cases, you must make a formal request to the bank for any additional payments or any withdrawals of excess payments, which will be then approved or rejected by the bank.

Flexi-loan—This is a newer product offered to give borrowers more flexibility. Flexi-loans would give you the flexibility to make additional payments and withdrawals as per your needs. The additional payments would reduce the interest you would need to pay and this in turn helps reduce the loan tenure. On the flip side, making withdrawals of any additional payments would then increase the interest and tenure. Take note though that flexi-loans usually require a monthly service fee, which is something conventional loans do not have. Therefore, for this product to be really useful, you need to make additional payments whenever possible, otherwise you may be better off with a conventional loan.

Base Lending Rate (BLR)

This is the base interest rate used by financial institutions when calculating the interest to be repaid for property loans. Financial institutions are free to set their own BLR but it is set based on the Overnight Policy Rate (OPR), which is determined by Bank Negara Malaysia (BNM) on a quarterly basis.

It is uncommon to find financial institutions with different BLR, due to the stiff competition between banks to sell their products, but it is advisable to check on the BLR rather than assume it is the same across the board.

At the point of writing, BLR is 6.60% for majority of the financial institutions in Malaysia.

Interest Rates

Interest rate is the rate that the financial institution will use to calculate the interest you need to pay each month. Interest rates are usually stated for a yearly or per annum (p.a.) basis but is usually calculated on a daily rest basis. Daily rest means interest is calculated on a daily basis and added to the outstanding amount on a monthly basis. For property loans, financial institutions offer two types of interest calculations, which are variable and fixed interest rates.

Variable interest rates—This is the most common type of interest rate being offered. The financial institutions usually offer interest rates that are based on the BLR and a spread. These are usually the best interest rates on offer at any given time, but as they are variable, the financial institutions are protected should the OPR be increased by BNM, as they can raise the BLR accordingly.

For example, you may be offered a loan with interest rate of BLR -2.00%. The spread in this case is "-2.00%". So, assuming the BLR is 6.60%, that would be the interest rate you are being offered is effectively 6.60%-2.00% = 4.60%. It is important that you also know that the spread does not always have to be negative. There have been instances in the past where financial institutions have offered loans with positive spreads, such as BLR + 0.50%.

Fixed interest rates—Fixed interest rates mean that the interest rate you pay is fixed over the tenure of the loan unless you decide to restructure it with the consent of the financial institution. The interest rates on offer for fixed interest rate loans are always higher than that of variable interest rate loans. This is as the financial institutions need to consider the potential risk of loss of income should the OPR be increased by BNM, at which time you would profit from having no change in your loan interest rates. However, in cases where the OPR is reduced by BNM, then the financial institutions would make more profit and you would lose out.

Tenure

The tenure is the maximum time period of the loan. It however, does not mean that you can only complete payment of the loan earlier. The tenure is used with other factors to determine the monthly installment that you would need to pay.

Lock-in Period

A lock-in period is the period within the loan tenure when you would be charged a penalty should you decide to settle your loan. You need to know how long the lock-in period lasts, and what would be the penalty you would need to pay if you decide to settle your loan within the lock-in period.

Other People's Money

This is a strategy where a person with no (or very little) money but is a savvy investor partners a person with money but is not a savvy investor.

If you are someone who knows how to invest and what to invest in, but just does not have the money, then you need to go out and find someone who has the money but for whatever reason cannot or does not invest. This is similar to investing in a mutual fund, where the investor contributes money for the fund manager to invest. So, as long as you are good at investing, you can be someone else's property manager.

On the other hand, if you have the money, then you could also look to partner with a savvy property investor to help you generate better returns that you would achieve on your own.

Lease Options

Lease options is an advanced financing strategy, which consists of two parts, the lease and the option. It is only applicable in specific circumstances but is widely practiced around the world in countries such as the UK, Australia and New Zealand. The lease is the part where the buyer actually leases the property from the seller for a fixed period of time. The option is the part where the buyer has the option but not the obligation to buy the property at an agreed price at a future time.

Should you decide to use this strategy, it would allow you to control the property without having to buy it until you decide to do so. To know more about this strategy, you can read *"Step by Step Guide to Lease Options—No Mortgage, No Deposit, No Problem"* by Vincent Wong and John Lee.

5) Lone rangers don't win . . . period.

Surround yourself with people who want you to win!

As with many aspects in life, property investment is not something you can do successfully without a team supporting you. All successful property investors have their respective teams to support them in all aspects of their transactions. And it is very important that you surround yourself with people who want you to win.

You should have the following members in your team

- Lawyer
- Mortgage Banker or Broker
- Real Estate Agent or Negotiator
- Tax Consultant
- Mentor or Coach

Lawyer

It is very important that you must have a lawyer in your team. You should not be pound wise and penny foolish by not appointing a lawyer. The simple reason is that all property transactions are legal transactions and you need as much legal advice as possible.

You need to be sure that your interests are protected in any contract that is drawn up and you need to be sure that the other party in the contract does not put in a clause or condition that puts you in a negative position.

Also, should any disputes happen, you will already have a lawyer who is already up to speed on the situation and ready to support you. This is definitely much better than to go scrambling around for legal advice when time is of the essence.

Mortgage Banker or Broker

Having a mortgage banker or broker who is on your team will also support your investments. Although you may know the basic strategies on how to prepare your loan applications, you definitely would not know as much as a good mortgage banker or broker.

They would be able to give you advice on your application, and if they think you are ready to apply for a new loan. It is in their interest to get your loan approved as they are usually paid by commissions. If you are a good client with a good history of repayment, they would definitely prioritize your application.

Real Estate Agent or Negotiator

Having a real estate agent or negotiator working for your team has also great benefits. These real estate professionals are going through many deals each day. And if you have them on your team, you would be able to get deals that suit you identified much faster.

Once you have an agent or negotiator who knows exactly what you are looking for, then you could take action very quickly once a deal comes along.

Tax Consultant

This is a team member who you may not need when you are starting off but may need when you have built a sizable investment portfolio. It is very important to know that not paying tax can have very severe penalties. So to ensure you are paying what you need to pay and not more, you would need the help of a tax consultant. It would be a small price to pay rather than to file your taxes incorrectly and get penalized in the future.

Mentor or Coach

Everyone should have a mentor or coach if they want to be successful. Even the most successful athletes in the world have coaches and mentors. A mentor or a coach is not there to take action for you, but is there to guide you and hold you accountable to your plans. Someone who can push you and motivate you that you constantly move towards your goals.

A mentor or coach will ensure you take action as you have planned, let you know when you are going off track and also help provide feedback when you are facing challenges or when you are reviewing the actions that you have taken.

6) Now you're ready to S.P.E.N.D!

5 Simple Steps to doing a deal—Search, Prepare, Eliminate, Negotiate, Do the Deal

After getting to know the basics of property investments, now comes the time to take action. It is very important to know that no matter how much you learn theoretically, there is no substitute for practical experience. You may still make mistakes along the way, but I am very sure that with the investment you have put into your education and the team that you have built around you, you would not make any critical mistakes. It is also important that you go through the steps and avoid taking shortcuts. Taking shortcuts may cause you to miss details that could come back to haunt you in the future.

The 5 simple steps to doing a deal are as follows

S—Search for Leads
P—Prepare a Shortlist
E—Eliminate by Qualification
N—Negotiate
D—Do the Deal

S: Search for Leads

Searching for property is the first real action you need to take. You should start buy listing down a criteria that you will use in your search. Some basic criteria that you should use are as follows . . .

- General location
- Budget
- Property type
- Property size
- Facilities
- Accessibility

General Location

What would your desired general location be? Would you want something close to where you live so you can easily manage the property? Or would you want a more mature and dense location? Deciding this will already help narrow your search significantly. Having too broad a scope will make your search longer and harder.

In general, a more mature and dense location will provide a bigger and better market for you irrespective if you decide to rent or sell. However, if you are unable to manage the property well then it may be better for you to go for a property that is nearer to home and therefore more convenient to manage.

Budget

Next is a very important thing, which is your budget. You need to set a reasonable budget based on your financial foundations and the market prices of the properties in your preferred location. Your financial foundation will determine what you can afford. If you cannot afford any property in your preferred location, then it is better to look somewhere else.

If the market values are within what you can afford, then you can continue narrowing your search. It is important to keep looking for value in any property that you want to invest in. The advice from many property millionaires is for you to earn when you buy and not when you sell. Always look to buy below market value as to already make profit at the point of purchase.

You need to define your budget prior to shortlisting as it only makes sense to shortlist properties that are within your budget. You can always look for properties that are marketed as slightly above your budget as you may succeed in negotiating the price down to meet your budget.

When preparing your budget, you must also put aside some funds to pay for incidental costs, such as legal fees and stamp duties, and also for any repairs or renovations that may be required for the property that you purchase.

Property Type

Knowing the property type you would like to invest in is also important. This will be determined based on the strategy that you are using. Here are some suggestions based on the strategies that were shared in the earlier chapter "The Property Millionaire Game Plan".

Buy before construction and sell upon completion

Any property type works for this strategy as long as there is demand for that property type within its location. Residential properties (especially apartments or condominiums) are much easier to sell or let than commercial, so if you are new or have limited financial strength, then go for apartments or condominiums.

Buy for Capital Appreciation

You should buy landed properties if you decide to use this strategy as they have the best potential for capital appreciation. Houses are the best for this strategy as they appreciate very well and rental returns are usually not very good. Commercial properties do appreciate in value very well, especially in mature areas but as the rental returns are very good, you may prefer to rent them out for cash flow instead of selling for capital gains.

Flipping

Apartments or condominiums are usually the best for this strategy. You would want a property that is in high demand to enable you to sell quickly after purchasing the property. Also, it is easier to sell low to medium cost properties than it is to sell high cost or luxury properties. However, you could also decide to go for other types of residential property as long as there is a high demand for the property in its location.

Buying to rent

Commercial properties are the best for this strategy as rental returns are very good. However, as the entry cost is very high you may want to start off with residential properties. Small apartments or condominiums are the best residential properties for this strategy. Studio or one room apartments usually have the highest demand and best rental returns in mature and dense locations. Apartments that have three rooms may be suitable for families in sub-urban areas.

Renting to Multiple Occupants

This strategy is best to be used for three room apartments or condominiums that are nearby colleges or universities. By renting out each room in the apartment separately, you can get higher rent in return for the tenants, who are usually students, needing only to manage their own rooms and not the whole apartment.

Property Size

It is important to know your target market when deciding on the best size for the property that you want. If your target market is young adults who are still single, then the smaller the unit the better. It is quite common now for young adults to rent or buy studio apartments, where they have personal privacy. It is unlikely that a young single adult rents or buys a three room apartment for themselves.

On the other hand, if you decide that you would like to rent or sell to families then you may need to look for larger property with at least two or three rooms. However, you need to note that if the property is too large, you may find it difficult to either let / sell the property or get good rental / selling price as your prospective tenants / buyers will only pay for what they need.

Facilities

Another criteria that will help you narrow your search is to identify facilities that you would want to have for your investment property. These facilities should be a value add and attractive for your target market. For example, 24 hour security is very much desired for safety reasons. Covered parking is also in demand for convenience reasons. Sufficient parking lots is also becoming quite an important factor as most families now have at least two cars.

You need to assess which facilities that are considered as basic requirements and which are facilities that are good to have. This is subject to the type of property that you are going for as high-end properties would definitely need 24 security, covered parking and at least two parking lots, whereas low to medium-end properties may only need 24 security and two parking lots.

Accessibility

Easy access to highways and major roads is a very attractive selling point for your property. I am sure everyone enjoys having the convenience of easy accessibility. This would be important in sub-urban residential areas which are further away from commercial and industrial centers as people would want to be able to travel smoothly between their place of residence and their place of work.

In very mature and densely populated locations, public transportation is a significant factor. Having a nearby train station or bus stop would be very much preferred. For example, a property that has a LRT station within 500m would definitely be preferred over another that is 2km away.

P: Prepare a Shortlist

This step is where you do your homework in preparation for your property purchase. Once you have come up with your search criteria, then you can start the next process, which is to prepare a shortlist of specific units that fit your criteria. From this shortlist then you can start eliminating less desirable properties before you start negotiations for the properties that you really want. There are two common ways to do this, which are either you do it by yourself or by getting your real estate agent / negotiator to do it for you.

You must remember that property investments is a numbers game. Most of the times, you will need to have a few properties shortlisted in order to land a deal. It is very unlikely that you will always shortlist one property and that property ends up as a deal. Therefore, it is also important that you be patient and persevere when preparing your shortlist.

Shortlisting Yourself

Shortlisting units by yourself is very easy nowadays with the internet and the many websites that have been set up specifically for advertising properties for sale and for rent. However, it does take up some time as you would need to search for a property that meets your criteria.

Shortlisting by your Real Estate Agent / Negotiator

Shortlisting by your Real Estate Agent / Negotiator is good in cases where you have little time to do the shortlisting. However, you should have already built a good relationship with your agent or negotiator if you really want good deals. What you need to understand is that agents / negotiators need to earn profit from each transaction through commissions. Unless you are a frequent client or are perceived to be a serious buyer who can close the deal very fast, they have very little motivation to give you a deal where they gain less profit.

E: Eliminate by qualification

The process of elimination is one where you qualify the properties in your shortlist to see if they really fit your criteria. Sometimes, there is information that is not shared or incorrectly shared that may cause you to change your mind, so you need to be rather thorough in qualifying the properties on your shortlist.

Most of the time, you will need to personally view the property that you have shortlisted. By personally viewing, you can check out the condition of the property plus identify any additional positive or negative points that may help you make up your mind. For example, you may not have realized that there is a LRT station nearby, which is a positive point, or you may not have known that there is a high-tension electricity cable running just beside the property, which is a negative point.

Also, you could check with a valuer or banker on the market valuation of the property. Sometimes, sellers want to sell their property over the market value, which may not be what you want.

N: Negotiate

Serious negotiations should only start after you have completed your shortlist. After the process of searching and shortlisting, you should already be very sure of what you want. This is important as once you reach this stage you may need to make decisions very quickly to lock in deals. If you can negotiate the price to be equal to or lower than your budget, then go ahead and transact. If you delay, you may lose out to someone else who was faster in taking action.

However, there are occasions when you need to be patient and persistent. For example, an owner is holding out for something just above your budget. And you have found out from your agent that the owner has been trying to sell for the past one year unsuccessfully. If you follow-up after a few months, the owner may decide to lower his asking price to meet your budget.

D: Do the Deal

Once you and the owner have agreed the terms and conditions for the transaction, then it is time for you to go ahead and do the deal. The transaction consists of three main parts, which are the Offer to Purchase, Sales and Purchase Agreement and Loan Process.

Offer to Purchase

The offer to purchase is made once you have agreed the terms and conditions with the seller. The offer to purchase should be a formal document that confirms your interest to purchase the said property and the terms and conditions that you and the seller have agreed. This document will then need to be passed to the lawyers to be used as a basis for the Sales and Purchase Agreement.

At this time, you would also be asked to pay an earnest deposit to confirm your interest. This earnest deposit should not be paid directly to the seller but should be paid to a third-party stakeholder such as the real estate agent / negotiator or a lawyer acting for you. This is to safeguard your interests should the process breakdown before the sales and purchase agreement process is completed.

Sales and Purchase Agreement

The Sales and Purchase Agreement is prepared by the lawyers appointed by the seller and yourself based on the offer to purchase that was prepared earlier. This is a very important document and will be the basis to discuss and disputes that may arise after the agreement is signed by both parties.

At this time, you would need to put a down payment of 10% less the earnest deposit that you have paid when you made the offer to purchase. This money will be paid to the seller through your lawyer after you have signed the agreement.

At the same time, you will then need to pay legal fees and stamp duty to your lawyer. The legal fees are calculated based on a guideline mandated by the Bar Council of Malaysia and the stamp duty for the sales and purchase agreement is calculated based on regulations under the purview of the Inland Revenue Board (or Lembaga Hasil Dalam Negeri, LHDN). You should have already planned this as part of your budget as discussed in another chapter.

Throughout the sales and purchase process, you should keep in close contact with your lawyer. This is to ensure that the process is going on smoothly. Once the process is complete, you will receive the keys to your property.

Loan Process

This part applies only if you are financing your property purchase using a loan from a financial institution. However, you should start this process as soon as possible, once you have decided on your property purchase. It is best for you to already have a loan offer letter in hand before you sign the sales and purchase agreement. This is to minimize your risk of defaulting on the purchase should your loan application be unexpectedly rejected. You can also request to put in a clause into the Offer to Purchase document that the Sales and Purchase Agreement is subject to upon your loan application being approved.

Loan Application

Applying for a loan is quite a simple process as the sales staff for financial institutions are always very helpful to potential customers. What you need to do is identify the loan product that best suits you from the various products being offered. It is advisable for you to "shop around" for the best loan product.

Once you have decided on which loan product suits you best, you then approach the sales staff of the financial institution to make your application. At this time, you will need to have supporting documents, such as income statements and bank statements, ready to be submitted together with your application. You can make applications to more than one financial institution as long as the products suit your requirements.

Letter of Offer

Once your application is approved, you would then receive a Letter of Offer. This letter of offer would contain all the terms and conditions that are being offered to you. You need to closely review the letter of offer before signing it. The details of the things you need to review have been covered in a different chapter. Once you have reviewed the terms and conditions, and are comfortable with them, then go ahead and sign the letter of offer.

Loan Agreement

After you have signed the letter of offer, then letter will then need to be passed to your lawyer to prepare the loan agreement. The thing to note here is that financial institutions in Malaysia require your lawyer to be a panel lawyer for them to be allowed to prepare a loan agreement between yourself and them.

Once you have signed the loan agreement, then the parts of the loan process that require your direct involvement are completed.

Loan Disbursement

The Loan Disbursement takes place after the Sales and Purchase Agreement has been signed. As mentioned before, this process does not require your direct involvement and will be coordinated by the lawyers and the banks involved.

Once disbursement takes place, then you would be required to start paying the bank the monthly installments. The financial institution will advise you accordingly when the disbursements take place.

7) Tenants: An investor's best friend

Wouldn't you love someone who pays for your property?

Now once you have purchased a property, and you think having a tenant is a good idea, here are some things you should know about having tenants. Everyone hopes to get the secret to having good tenants. There actually is no real secret on how you can get good tenants. What is most important is that you invest the required time and effort to find them. And in cases where you got tenants who did not live up to your expectations, you need to find the right way to coax them to leave so you can start looking for new tenants.

Finding Tenants

Finding tenants is like finding the right dress or the right shirt. You need to shop around and take your time to find the right one. Giving yourself sufficient time to evaluate and interview prospective tenants is actually giving yourself sufficient opportunity to find the best tenants possible. It is important that you do not rush into finding tenants. On one hand, you hope to have positive cash flow as soon as possible, but you also need to balance that against the risk of getting a tenant who actually is in financial trouble and cannot pay you after the first month.

It is very important that you take the time to interview each prospective tenant to get to know them better. You should try to find out a bit about their background. For example, you can ask them what they do for a living. Are they employees from a multi-national company? Or are they entrepreneurs running their own businesses? Or are they students in the nearby university? Knowing their background will help you prepare to manage them in the future.

Similar to when you are buying a property, it is good to build up a shortlist of prospective tenants before you commit to any one tenant. Of course, in cases where you have limited choices, then you should go with what you think is the best choice at that point of time. Waiting for the right candidate is also a choice you can make, especially if the prospective tenants make you uncomfortable. You should remember that if you need to balance getting a good tenant and getting positive cash flow as soon as possible.

Tenancy Agreement

Once you have identified the tenant that you think is the best fit, go ahead to discuss and agree with the tenant the various terms and conditions. When you and your future tenant have agreed terms, then you should then ensure that a tenancy agreement is put in place. Similar to a sales and purchase agreement, this can be used to settle any disputes that may arise in the future. In Malaysia, you should ensure that the agreement is stamped, so it is accepted as a legally binding document. This is to protect your interest and also the interest of your tenant.

Be Firm and Fair

Tenant management is really like people management in any organization. Whether you own a business or if you are working as an employee managing others, the concepts behind managing tenants is the same. What is most important is that you are both firm and fair.

You need to be firm right from the start and to keep to the terms and conditions of the tenancy agreement. For example, if rent is to be paid before the 5th of every month, then you need to follow-up to ensure that your tenant is paying on time. For a start, you may want to send a reminder a few days before the due date so the tenant is not given any room to make excuses later on.

You also need to be fair to your tenant. There will be different scenarios that come up when your tenant may come to you for help. And should this happen you need to be fair to your tenant. For example, if you happen to be going on a holiday when the tenant is due to pay you rent, you cannot expect the tenant to pay you before you leave for the holiday without prior agreement. In this case, you should inform the tenant that you will be collecting the rent once you return from your holiday and keep to this commitment.

Once you are sure that you have a good tenant, then maybe you would want to reward your tenant from time to time. For example, if you won a TV in a lucky draw, maybe you could replace the old TV that you provided to your tenant. Simple acts go a long way in keeping tenants happy.

Rent to Buy

Here is an advanced strategy that you can use to manage your tenants and also get rental premiums if market rent is unable to cover your monthly loan repayments. This is similar to the Lease Option strategy covered in a different chapter, but in this case, you are renting out your property to a tenant and giving your tenant the option to buy in the future. So, in this case, you are actually getting a tenant-buyer instead of just a tenant.

By doing this, you actually are in a position to negotiate for better rent, which can be used to offset the future down payment that would be made by your tenant-buyer. At the same time, your tenant-buyer would be motivated to take care of the property as if it is his/her own, since your tenant-buyer has the option to purchase it in the future, with the down payment offset by the premium rent. To know more about this strategy, you can read *"Step by Step Guide to Lease Options—No Mortgage, No Deposit, No Problem" by Vincent Wong and John Lee.*

8) And now . . . to prosperity and beyond!

How to keep growing your wealth over and over again . . .

Once you have successfully completed your first property deal, and your tenants are moved in and paying their rent, then it is time to shift your focus to keep the momentum going. Continue investing, firstly in yourself and then subsequently in more properties and you are on your way to prosperity and beyond!

It is very important that you keep investing in your education and knowledge. There are various ways of doing this such as

- Reading books or e-books
- Listening to audio-books
- Reading magazines and newspapers
- Attending webinars, seminars and conferences
- Attending networking events
- S.P.E.N.D at least once a year

Once you have the momentum going then you can start to prepare for your next property deal. If it helps, go through the steps as covered in this book again until you are familiar.

Reading Books or e-books

Reading books or e-books is a very good way to keep on expanding your horizons and learning new strategies. You get to see different viewpoints from different people who have been successful. Also, you should read books covering differing aspects that will support your investment objectives. For example, if you think you need to work on having the correct mindset, then go out and get books that help you get your mindset right. Alternatively, if you think you need help with specific strategies for property investments, then go out and get those books.

Listening to audio-books

If you are more inclined to listening rather than reading, then go for audio-books. Nowadays there are many books that have been converted into audio-books to make it easier for those who prefer listening over reading. You should also consider going for audio-books this if you spend a lot of time driving. You can kill two birds with one stone by listening to audio-books while driving.

Reading Magazines and Newspapers

Reading magazines and newspapers allows you to keep expanding your horizons, learning new strategies and stay in tune with the changes in the market, environment and regulations. This is to ensure you do not get left behind due to changes in market trends. You should do this every day to keep your momentum going. Magazines and newspapers are the best at keeping you up to date, as they are periodical and the content is always revised to ensure it is up to date.

Attending webinars, seminars and conferences

Attending webinars, seminars and conferences on property investments allows you to keep up to date on the environment and strategies in a more direct manner. Similar to reading magazines and newspapers, this ensures you do not get left behind due to changes in market trends. Listening to what industry experts have to say will put you ahead of the game. Webinars are shorter events which you can fit into your daily schedule, whereas you may need to plan ahead to attend seminars and conferences. Either way, you must invest in this to keep your investing foundations strong.

Attending networking events

Attending networking events allows you to meet up with like-minded people and discuss topics that are relevant to you. You can take advantage of such events to look for investment partners. Alternatively you can look for someone who may have experience in a specific type of investment strategy that you are planning to use to learn from. At the same time, you can also share your own experience with others and even inspire others to keep their momentum going.

S.P.E.N.D at least once a year

Doing a deal once a year is a sure and steady way to becoming a property millionaire. It gives you enough time to do the deal and prepare for the next one without compromising on your foundations. It is also the best way to learn as there is no substitute for practice. Analyze your actions through your transaction and make improvements wherever necessary.

Closing Words

First and foremost, I'd like to thank you for purchasing and reading this book! To further add value to your investing journey, I am giving you the excel templates that I use for FREE! Just visit the following link to download. www.9to5propertymillionaire.com/excel_template

Included are templates I use for

- Tracking Net Worth on a monthly basis
- Determining Monthly Cash Flow
- Mortgage Calculator to calculate the monthly installments required when taking up a loan—plus feature to calculate potential savings by making Extra Payments
- Transaction Cost Calculator to calculate required costs needed up front when making a property purchase

As with any book, there is only so much that I can write about. I wish I could write more but I also do not want to have a book that is too thick and boring that puts you to sleep. I prefer books that are concise, straight to the point and still informative. I hope this book has sparked your interest and inspires you to seek more knowledge.

I am more than willing to help you on your journey towards becoming the next 9 to 5 property millionaire. All I ask is that you give your full commitment to your own journey to success . . . do we have a deal?

Please do keep in touch with me by visiting and liking my Facebook page https://www.facebook.com/9to5propertymillionaire.

Wishing you the very best in your investments!

About the author

B K Khoo was an employee just like many others out there. When he first started working in 2005, he was focused on climbing the corporate ladder and did not take investments seriously. All this changed when he lost his job on his wedding day as the company he had been working for 4 years filed for bankruptcy in 2009. From that day on, he realized that having a job was no guarantee in life. Gone were the days of old where employees could spend their whole careers in the same company. He needed to take action to ensure a brighter future for his family.

After getting a new job, BK concentrated again on climbing the corporate ladder, but this time around he also started investing in himself to prepare himself for investing. He spent a lot of time reading books on different types of investments and also attended different seminars to build up his foundations. After that, he decided that property investments were the most suitable type of investment to complement his job. Success in his job allowed him to invest more in himself and in property, which became his foundation to create a brighter future for his family.

Fast forward to 2013, BK was for the second time, made redundant, due to a restructuring in the company he was working for. This time however, he was ready for it and has decided not to become an employee again. He is passionate about inspiring other employees to start investing while still on their jobs, irrespective of whether you love or hate your job. He hopes to share the message that your job and investments should complement each other to bring you great success.